Stevia
Rebaudiana

Nature's *sweet* ∧ Secret

David Richard

No part of this book may be reproduced in any form without the written consent of the publisher.

Stevia Rebaudiana: Nature's Sweet Secret is written for informational purposes only. It is not intended to diagnose or prescribe any medical condition nor to replace common sense and reasonable caution in consuming Stevia products. Neither the author nor the publisher is responsible for defects in the manufacturing, processing, or handling of Stevia products.

Published by Vital Health Publishing
Ridgefield, CT
www.vitalhealthbooks.com

Copyright © 1996 by Vital Health Publishing
Second Edition, 1998
Third Edition, 1999

Design, Layout and Typesetting by Studio 2D, Champaign, IL
Printing by United Graphics, Mattoon, IL

Preface to the Third Edition

Since I first wrote this book, I have come to better understand the process of refining stevia leaves. I have also grown in my appreciation of the value of foods and herbs in their whole, unprocessed state. For these reasons, I am now able to see the advantages of stevia in its natural state (fresh leaves) or in minimally-processed extracts vs. purified stevioside or highly-refined extracts.

I continue to favor refined stevia extracts over artificial sweeteners because these extracts "filter down" a natural, edible substance while artificial sweeteners are largely "constructed" from chemically-pure, inedible substances. Yet I see that the nutritive problems in refined stevia extracts are similar to other highly-refined foods, sugar (sucrose) for instance. In both cases, complex nutrients are processed out of the end product while trace amounts of the extractive agents remain in it.

My preference, therefore, is toward the more natural forms of stevia: whole leaves, green powders and simple, "crude" extracts from the whole leaves.

A step in this direction might be to no longer bleach the stevia extracts in the refining process. Bleaching is a non-essential, cosmetic process anyway. Unbleached stevia extracts might be likened to unbleached flour. While not "whole-grain," they would nonetheless be healthier than their bleached cousins. Bleached and highly-refined powdered stevia extracts can be easily distinguished by their pure white color. The more unrefined products are a creamy beige with a hint of their original green.

Beyond this, the goal of a simple extractive process needs to be pursued in order to retain the full spectrum of soluble nutrients as well as all of the sweet glycosides of the stevia leaves. Superior flavor characteristics need to come from superior agricultural methods and conditions, preferable organic, and not through chemical isolation and purification techniques.

My desire is the influence you toward improved health. I trust that this information will allow you to make healthier choices and insure that these choices are made available to you.

We need to learn from nature and honor the traditional usage of herbs like stevia. For our health is enhanced, as individual and as a culture, by nature's roots, twigs and leaves.

Acknowledgements

I would like to thank Jeffrey Goettemoeller of Prairie Oaks Seeds for his efforts in compiling and writing chapter 8 – Growing Your Own Stevia. Jeffrey's recipe book, *Stevia Sweet Recipes: Sugar-Free – Naturally!* (144 pp., $9.95) is also available from Vital Health Publishing and will be re-published in both a Spanish edition (164 pp. $10.95) and an expanded English edition (200 pp., $12.95) this fall.

Special thanks also to Mark Langan of Mulberry Creek Herb Farm whose extensive horticultural experience with Stevia has been most helpful. The plants you sent me are healthy and well-rooted, Mark, and the leaves taste fresh and sweet!

I am also grateful for the recipes that were submitted by health food store employees and nutritionists to help people get started in cooking with Stevia extracts and powders.

Finally, my thanks to Gretchen of Studio 2D with whom it has been a pleasure to work, and to Joan, my assistant, who spent many hours patiently typing and editing this manuscript.

Table of Contents

CHAPTER ONE

The Secret of Stevia

S tevia Rebaudiana is a small shrub native to portions of Northeastern Paraguay and adjacent sections of Brazil. It flourishes in the sandy soil of this elevated terrain and may grow to a height of 80 cm when it is fully mature. While native Indians of the Guarani Tribe appear to have used the leaves of this herb as a sweetener since pre-Columbian times, it was not until 1887 when a South American natural scientist named Antonio Bertoni first "discovered" it.

Bertoni originally designated this plant as Eupatorium Rebaudianum Bertoni (related to boneset), but later reassigned it to the genus Stevia, (1905). It is estimated that there are over 80 species of Stevia known to grow wild in North America and perhaps as many as two hundred additional species native to South America. Of these, only Stevia Rebaudiana and another now-extinct species appear to posses the natural sweetness which are their distinguishing characteristics.

The sweet secret of Stevia lies in a complex molecule called Stevioside which is a glycoside composed of glucose, sophorose and steviol. It is this complex molecule and a number of other related compounds that account for Stevia Reubaudiana's extraordinary sweetness. The Stevia herb in its natural form is approximately 10 to 15 times sweeter than common table sugar. Extracts of Stevia in the form of Steviosides can range anywhere from 100 to 300 times sweeter than table sugar. And best of all, Stevia does not affect blood sugar metabolism according to most experts. Some studies even report that Stevia reduces plasma glucose levels in normal adults.

Why has Stevia been kept such a secret? How was it used historically? How is it grown? What are its pharmacological and nutritive benefits? How is it used around the world today? Why was it kept off the market for so many years? Are steviosides safe? And finally, how can we use Stevia in cooking and preparing our foods each day? These are the questions that this book will try to answer. Hopefully it will give you some insight into this wonderfully sweet herb and allow you to make the decision of how and why to include it in your daily diet.

CHAPTER TWO

A Brief History

As mentioned previously, it was Antonio Bertoni who first discovered Stevia in 1887. Originally considered a part of the daisy family, it was re-assigned to the chrysanthemum (Asteraceae) family in the Eupatorieae Tribe in 1905. Bertoni learned of the herb and its curious sweetening properties from the Guarani Paraguayan Indians, Mestizos and others who had used it to sweeten bitter beverages, particularly maté. Stevia was known locally as Caa'-ehe or Kaa'-he-E which can be translated as "sweet-herb" or "honeyleaf." By the turn of the century, it was well-known and widely used by herbalists in Paraguay as a sweetener in teas.

By 1901, a man named C. Gosling, who was the British Consul at Asuncion, was able to write:

This plant, which has been known to the Indians (Guarani) since a hundred years or more and whose secret has as usual been so faithfully guarded by them, grows in the Highlands of Amambai and near the source of the River Monday. . . . The leaves are small and the flower still more diminutive, and the Indians call it Caa'-ehe, meaning sweet herb, because of its sweetness, a few leaves being sufficient to sweeten a strong cup of tea, giving also a pleasant aromatic flavor.

In an article entitled "Composition of Empatorium Rebaudiana (Stevia)" written for the June 1909 edition of Chemist and Druggist, Karl

Dieterich wrote that the sweet plant of Paraguay, also known as honey yerba, is used in an area where it is found to sweeten maté. He also noted that the species had been successfully cultivated in Paraguay by 1909.

Two French chemists named Bridel and Lavieille began to unravel the secret of Stevia in 1931 with exploratory extraction work on Stevia Rebaudiana leaves. Their research yielded a pure white crystalline compound which they named "Stevioside" which was recovered at a six percent yield. They found this substance to be 300 times sweeter than table sugar and without apparent toxic effects in various experimental animals.

In 1941, because of the scarcity of sugar and other sweeteners in England due to the German submarine blockade, a substitute sweetener was sought out which could be cultivated in the British Isles. The Director of the Royal Botanical Gardens at Kew commissioned an R. Melville to research Stevia as a likely possibility. Melville's report shows that he believed Stevia Rebaudiana could be just the substitute for which they were looking.

Melville reported:

(that the leaves of Stevia) have long been used by the natives of Paraguay for sweetening their maté and as a general sweetening agent. Their use has been suggested for sweetening beer, tobacco and instead of sugar in drinks for hot climates. Later, the possibility of employing the leaves or the extracted sweet principals was considered for sweetening diabetic foods. . . . Two or three leaves are enough to sweeten a cup of tea or coffee.

In the same private report, Melville also noted that the leaves of the Stevia Plant may be kept indefinitely in the dried condition, added whole or powdered to tea or coffee, and powdered leaves could be used for sweetening stewed fruit and other dishes without the necessity of separating the sweet principles.

The Director at Kew apparently took Mr. Melville's report seriously, for within a year, seeds were sent from Paraguay to some of the milder areas of the U.K. where cultivation experiments were started. Newspaper articles reported that these experiments were successful in Cornwall and Devon, where the equivalent of two tons of sugar per acre were shown to be possible to produce. However, for unknown reasons, the project was set aside and largely forgotten in the aftermath of the war.

In an unpublished manuscript written to the National Agricultural Institute of Paraguay in 1945, L.A. Gattoni was the first to advocate the development of a Stevioside industry in Paraguay. In addition, he outlined a commercial production process to create an extract which was superior to saccharine.

The work of Bridel and Lavielle was continued in 1952 by a group of researchers at the National Institute of Arthritis and Metabolic Diseases, a branch of the U.S. Public Health Service in Bethesda, Maryland. They both increased the yield of Steviosides to 7% based on an advanced extraction procedure and revealed the main features of the large and complicated Stevioside molecule. Their research also confirmed that Stevioside is the sweetest natural product yet found, that it is non-nitrogenous, and yet that it contains glucose. Ironically, in an article commenting on this work, one of the researchers states that "Stevioside does not appear to have an immediate future as a sweetener" because "it is difficult to see how Stevioside could compete economically with such a cheap, *safe*, and well-established synthetic sweetener as saccharin." Such commentary leads one to wonder about the actual safety of today's "safe" synthetic sweeteners. I, myself, avoid them entirely.

In 1954, the Japanese began to study Stevia seriously and to grow it in hothouses in Japan. And in 1971, a Chinese researcher, Dr. Tei-fu-chen visited Paraguay where he became so interested in Stevia, that he applied for residency status in both Paraguay and Brazil. The non-chemical method of extraction recorded in the herbal manuscripts of the Chinese Emperors became the method of extraction for the Stevia product, and it removed both the undesirable color and bitter aftertaste from the Stevia leaves. Shortly after Chen started his studies in Stevia, the Japanese industry began to use it extensively to sweeten pickles, dried foods, dried sea foods, fish and meat products, soy sauce, fruit juices, soft drinks, frozen deserts, gum and low-calorie food.

Today, Stevia is grown and used around the world for its incredible sweetening properties. It has been studied for its potential beneficial effects on diabetics. It has been shown to retard the growth of plaque in the mouth and also to be anti-cariogenic. Dozens of studies have shown Stevia to be a safe product for human use, and it is currently being used extensively as a substitute for both sugar products and artificial sweeteners.

More information of Stevia's current usage around the world is available in Chapter 5.

CHAPTER THREE

Botany and Cultivation

Stevia Rebaudiana Bertoni, as I have noted, is a herbaceous perennial shrub native to the highlands of Paraguay, which also grows near the 25° S Latitude in Brazil and Argentina.

A member of the Compositae Family, it has many common names, including: Ca-a jhee, Caa-a yupe, Caa-jhe-he and Yerba Dulce. These can either be translated as "Honey-Leaf" or "Sweet-Herb," both of which are accurate descriptions of the remarkable sweetness of Stevia Rebaudiana leaves.

The Stevia plant grows to a maximum height of 24 inches in the wild while cultivated varieties have reached heights up to 36 inches. Stevia is a spindly plant with many branches and a simple paired leaf structure. The root system of the Stevia plant consists of fine roots which spread out near the surface of the soil and thicker roots which grow deeper into the soil.

Stevia grows wild primarily in the infertile acid sands or mucks which occur along the edge of marshes or in grassland communities with shallow water tables, yet it has shown itself to be adaptable to a variety of soil conditions. In terms of climate, Stevia grows naturally in a semi-humid, subtropical climate with a temperature range of 21°F to 110°F and an average temperature of 75°F. Local rainfall averages 55 inches per year which keeps the coarse-textured soil continuously moist, but not subject to prolonged inundation.

According to an Agronomy Report from the University of California of Davis, Stevia reproduces in the wild "by seed, crown division or the rooting of branches which lodge in the soil or are trampled by cattle." It typically grows from a shoot in the early spring to a full-flowering plant in the late summer and early fall. While the shoots usually die after maturing, new growth comes from tillering at the base of the plant. A period of rapid growth in the second half of the first growing season follows a much slower period of growth in the first half of the season. In subsequent seasons, the initial growth rate is somewhat more rapid. Because seed production is erratic, most of the plants growing in the wild are survivors from plants growing in the previous year.

Stevia has been successfully cultivated in many parts of the world, including not only South America, but also Japan, Korea, Taiwan, The Philippine Islands, Southeast Asia, Great Britain, Israel, California and Southern Ontario. By transplanting Stevia plants from their native habitat, in addition to grazing and harvesting activities, the natural occurrence of Stevia plants has been severely diminished.

Cultivated Stevia plants not only grow taller than their wild "cousins," they also produce more branches and a greater number of leaves. Because of seed fertility problems, most Stevia propagation is accomplished using plant cuttings or induction of seed primordia. Many growers start their Stevia plants indoors initially in order to improve their germination rates and increase the length of their growing season and then transplant the seedlings outdoors as early in the spring as possible in order to maximize growth and yield.

Studies have been performed to determine the effect of long and short day lengths on the growth of Stevia plants and their various constituents. Shorter days have been shown to promote flowering and seed fertility as in the Paraguayan flowering season of January to March (equivalent to our July to September period). Longer days have favored the development of new leaves and branches and the yield of sweet-tasting glycosides. Longer days also appear to increase gibberellin synthesis, plant growth hormones which will be discussed in greater detail in the next chapter.

It has been noted that cultivated Stevia does not compete well with weeds and needs to be densely-planted in order to avoid breakage in unsheltered areas due to the wind and rain. In this case, the closely-spaced plants help support and shelter each other. Some growers thin the Stevia plants out by transplantation after the first year when the plants are hardier and stronger, thereby allowing each plant to reach its full development potential. Stevia plants also require a continuously moist soil base which creates a negative susceptibility to drought conditions.

Stevia is typically harvested at the beginning of its flowering cycle when the leaf weight is the greatest and when the stevioside content is at its peak. Prior to this, the optimal range of temperature for growing Stevia is 15–38°C. It has also been confirmed that both leaf weight and Stevioside content are greatest in plants grown at the higher latitudes where summer days are the longest.

Stevioside yields of 6–12% have been commonly noted in cultivated Stevia leaves. On a per acre basis, one study showed a stevioside yield of 220 lbs. per acre with a sweetening power equivalent of approximately 28 tons/acre of table sugar!

One of the more recent studies has found some constituents of apparent value in the flowers of the Stevia plant, including Stevioside (.04%), Rebaudioside A (.21%), Jhanol (.18%) and Austroinulin (.08%).

CHAPTER FOUR

Metabolism and Pharmacology

W hile Stevia has primarily been used as a sweetener, it has also been investigated as an aid in regulating blood-sugar metabolism, as an anti-hypertensive agent, as a source of plant growth hormones and flavonoid glycosides, as a contraceptive agent and as an anti-bacterial substance. Some cautionary research has also been done which shows at least two of Stevia's metabolites to inhibit glycogenesis and oxidative phosphorylation in various testing situations. Other research has examined the possible anti-androgenic activity of extracts of Stevia and Stevia metabolites.

Much of the research performed on Stevia is preliminary with numerous contradictory results and conclusions. Because metabolites are often used as test substances, determining the exact human digestive and metabolic pathways of Stevia and Stevioside seems critically important. To date, no definitive study has made this determination. Much of the research has been based on extrapolations from rat metabolism studies which may not be valid in terms of human beings. Finally, it is interesting to note that some of the contradictory results in pharmacological testing may be due to inconsistencies in materials used. Crude Stevia decoctions and full-spectrum extracts have typically been ascribed broader pharmacological activity than isolated extracts or constituents of Stevia.

In terms of the rat metabolism studies on Stevia, the crude herb has been supposed to break down to its glycoside components, where the majority of attention has been focused. A 1980 study reported that two of these glycosides, Stevioside and Rebaudioside A, were both degraded to the aglycone, Steviol, by microflora taken from a rat's intestines. These same researchers later showed that Steviol, administered orally, was almost completely absorbed by live rats at the site of their cecum. However, human studies on Stevia metabolism are lacking, and extrapolation from these preliminary studies to human beings is questionable since human microflora differs from rat microflora and human conversion of Stevia to Steviol and its subsequent absorption has neither been studied nor proven. It should be noted that, in the many acute and long-term toxicity tests of Stevia and its sweet glycosides, there has been no indication of any toxicity or harm caused by these substances. A more detailed discussion of Stevia's safety can be found in Chapter 6.

A good deal more research has chemically analyzed the Stevia Rebaudiana plant and identified many of its organic constituents, including the sweet glycosides listed in the following chapter. In addition, several diterpenes and triterpenes have been separated from the leaves as have the plant sterols, β-sistosterol and Stigmasterol. A total of 31 essential oils have also been extracted from the leaves in addition to various tannins. A more curious reader should refer to the data in D. Kinghorn and D. Soejarto's 1985 paper entitled "Current Status of Stevioside as a Sweetening Agent for Human Use" which was published in Volume I of *Economic and Medicinal Plant Research*, by the Academic Press Inc. (London) Ltd.

The data supporting a hypoglycemic activity of Stevia or its extracts is equivocal. Perhaps using the Doctrine of Signatures, Herbalists in Brazil have "prescribed" decoctions or extracts of Stevia to regulate blood sugar levels for at least forty years. However, almost all of the research in support of this usage has been published in the form of abstracts with little detailed support. Other research has directly contradicted these results.

Most of the research favoring a hypoglycemic activity of Stevia has come from South America. One early study (Oviedo et al., 1970) showed a 35.2% reduction in blood sugar levels in 25 healthy adults based on an unspecified dosage of liquid Stevia extract. Another study in 1981 (Alvarez et al), showed "an accentuated hypoglycemic response" in 15 normal adults studies but failed to include detailed control data. A Japanese study by H. Suzuki and associates in 1977, based on a .5% addition of Stevioside to the diet of laboratory rats, showed a significant decrease in liver glycogen levels after two weeks which was not reflected in blood sugar levels until a decrease was observed four weeks into the test. It should be noted that .5% consists of a very high dietary intake of the super-sweet Stevioside portion of Stevia. Other Japanese researchers (Oshima, et al., 1986), in an effort to find "plant-origin hypoglycemic constituents . . . of promising activity," have isolated eight diterpenes, Sterebins A-H, one of which is closely related to austrinulin. Further research is underway in an effort to determine possible physiological activity.

On the other hand, several studies by Lee and co-workers (1979), Akashi and Yokoyama (1975) and Medon (1985) have shown no dose-related effects on blood glucose levels when either crude extracts of Stevia or Stevioside extracts were administered for up to 56 days. Another study on the isolated rat pancreas (Usami et al., 1980) concluded "Stevioside does not influence arginine-induced insulin and glucagon secretion in the perfused rat pancreas." Thus, while a possible relationship between Stevia and blood sugar levels has been suggested, the burden of proof is that this relationship is unlikely to exist. If it does exist, more research is needed to quantify its activity and define its mode of action.

There have also been several studies performed on Stevia and its extracts which may indicate some effects on the cardiovascular system, kidney functioning and blood pressure. Performed by M. S. Melis and co-workers at the University of San Paulo, Brazil (1985, 1991, 1992), these experiments support earlier research by Von Schmeling (1967) and Humboldt and Boeck (1979, 1981) which demonstrated "a marked decrease in mean arterial pressure and heart rate as well as diuresis" upon application of measured dosages of Stevia extract or Stevioside. In particular, these experiments noted an increase in the excretion of sodium and potassium by the kidneys which accompanied the decrease in blood pressure, and they postulated that Stevioside acts, in some way, as a calcium antagonist like the prescription drug, Verapamil. Again, however, more research is necessary before any firm conclusions can be drawn.

The Stevia plant has also been examined as a possible source of plant growth hormones or gibberellins and flavonoid glycosides. While the flavonoid levels were low in relation to the sweet glycoside levels, a 1983 study by Rajbhandari and Roberts (London University) showed that Stevia leaves contain caempferol, apignin, luteolin, quercitrin, two forms of quercitin, and centaureidin. In addition, a 1982 study at the University of Tokyo (Nagura et al) showed that several gibberellins could be produced from Steviol and its derivatives through metabolism by the fungus gibberella fujikuroi. Earlier, a 1976 study by Valio and Rocha had shown that Steviol alone demonstrated a gibberellin-like activity in spurring the growth of lettuce, cucumber and bean plants.

There has been some controversy over whether Stevia Rebaudiana and its extracts have any contraceptive effects. While an early research study (Planas and Kuc, 1968) claimed that Paraguay Indians used the herb as a contraceptive beverage and reported an anti-fertility effect in their experiments with male and female rats, no evidence of this activity has been found in any follow-up research. Quite the opposite, at least seven studies have shown that Stevia has no effect on animal fertility, and several studies have also shown that Stevia does not affect the rate of abnormalities in the offspring of Stevia-fed male and female rats.

Stevioside appears to be the sweetener of choice in toothpastes, mouthwashes and gums intended to decrease the incidence of dental caries. In an experiment to determine the effect of Stevioside on growth rates of the Streptoccocus mutans types of bacteria, Stevioside was shown to be a less favorable bacterial growth medium than either glucose, sucrose or fructose (Berry and Henry, 1981). In another study, Stevioside (0.5%) markedly suppressed the growth of both Streptococcus mutans and Lactobacillus plantarum. It also completely inhibited the growth of Lactobacillus Casei. However, in combination with glucose, the inhibition of S. mutans growth was only moderate. Finally, in combination with sucrose, no inhibitory effect was noted. Production of the harmful enzymes dextran sucrase and invertase from S-mutans was also reduced by Stevioside favorably in relationship to other sweeteners. Dextran sucrase production was reduced 18% by Stevioside, 10% by Glucose, 5% by Xylitol and 0% by Sorbitol. Stevioside inhibited invertase production 20%, while both sorbitol and xylitol showed no inhibitory activity (Yabu et al, 1977).

Some cautionary research (Kelmer Brecht et al., 1984) has been performed on Steviol, the aglycone of Stevioside, in relationship to glycogenesis and oxidative phosphorylation in the isolated mitochondria of the liver-fractions of test rats. This research shows that Steviol may inhibit both glycogenesis (glucose production) and oxidative phosphorylation (the conversion of food to energy) in this testing environment. However, since the metabolism of Stevia is only beginning to be understood, it is unlikely that Steviol ever arrives at the site where it may become detrimental. The basis of this statement is the fact that none of the short or long-term toxicity studies of Stevia and its by-products have shown any single or cumulative detrimental effects.

As we move toward a better understanding of Stevia and its effects on the body, it is likely that we will use more of its components in constructive ways. Also, scientists will undoubtedly strive to synthesize many of Stevia's valuable components, as they are already trying to do. For myself, I prefer to appreciate the mystery and wonder of this unique plant and use it in its whole form with all of its complex and complementary nutrients intact instead of using the isolated constituents of Stevia. In this way, I have come to better understand how I react to Stevia and how Stevia reacts to me.

CHAPTER FIVE

Stevia's Usage Around the World

From its humble and relatively obscure "discovery" in Paraguay at the turn of the century, Stevia has blossomed into a major export crop and is now cultivated in over a dozen countries world-wide. Stevia usage is even more widespread with nearly every industrialized country now consuming a portion of the world's Stevia crop. It is estimated that 650–700 tonnes of dried Stevia Rebaudiana Plants were used in 1981 to make Stevioside extracts.

The largest user remains Japan which began cultivating Stevia plants in hothouses in 1954. When the Japanese government banned certain artificial sweeteners due to health concerns in the late sixties, the use of Stevia as a natural alternative increased dramatically. Stevia's usage has also increased due to the health concerns of Japanese consumers toward sucrose, related to dental caries, obesity and diabetes. By 1987, a total of 1700 metric tonnes of Stevia leaves were harvested to yield an estimated 190 tonnes of Stevioside extract. By 1988, extracts of Stevia had captured 41%, by value, of the Japanese high-potency sweetener market. Most of this material was processed through eleven major Stevia manufacturers who have collectively formed the Stevia Association of Japan.

Japanese food processors use Stevia in a wide variety of applications. The major usage is surprisingly with salty foods where Stevioside has been shown to suppress the pungency of sodium chloride. This combination is common to the Japanese diet in such foods as pickled vegetables, dried seafoods, soy sauce and miso products. It is also used in beverages, including (until recently) the Japanese version of Diet Coke. Stevia has also been used in candies and gums, baked goods and cereals, yogurt and ice cream, ciders and teas, and toothpastes and mouthwashes. Of course, a significant portion of Japanese Stevia is consumed directly as a tabletop sweetener.

The Japanese have also pioneered the purification of Stevia extracts into other sweet-tasting glycosides besides Stevioside. These include: Rebaudiosides A, B, C, D and E; Dulcoside A and Steviolbioside. Rebaudioside A and E are particularly noteworthy since they have a more refined sweet taste than Stevioside with less of the characteristic bitter aftertaste. Many "recipes" and extractive processes for Stevia glycosides have been patented in Japan as well as combinations of Stevia with other natural and synthetic sweeteners. One common combination of sweeteners is Stevioside with the licorice extract, glycyrrhizin, which results in the improved taste qualities of both sweeteners.

Food technologists in Japan have also discovered a great deal of important information relative to Stevia's application in food processing. First of all, Stevioside and other extracts of Stevia are relatively stable during heat processing in comparison to other natural and synthetic supersweeteners. One study in 1977, showed very low decomposition levels in a variety of pH conditions when Stevioside was heated to 100°C for up to twenty-four hours. It has also been shown that Stevia extracts are non-fermenting and do not contribute to the browning reaction of cooked or baked goods as do many natural sweeteners. Another advantage of Stevia is that it does not form precipitates in an acid solution, making it a compatible sweetener for carbonated soft drinks. Finally, many formulations and mixtures of Stevia extracts have been developed in order to highlight specific taste profiles such as a product developed for frozen desserts which require light but steady sweetness. In this and many other industrial applications, Stevia extracts and Stevioside have shown themselves to be versatile sweetening ingredients.

Stevioside has also been approved as a food additive in South Korea and is widely available in China, Taiwan and Malaysia. In China, teas are made from the Stevia leaves which are recommended "for increasing the appetite, as a digestant, for losing weight, for keeping young and as a sweet tasting low-caloric tea."

In Paraguay and Brazil, Stevia is widely tauted as a remedy for diabetes, although current scientific evidence does not adequately support this claim. It is also used extensively in black teas and herbal teas as well as other food applications. Once again, a significant portion is used in these countries as a tabletop sweetener.

With the re-emergence of Stevia into the U.S. market, numerous possibilities exist for the development of Stevia food products. However, the hurdle of obtaining GRAS status for Stevia as a food additive remains a formidable one. The health food industry has been striving to overcome this hurdle since 1991 when a Stevia Committee was formed under the auspices of the American Herbal Products Association. Thus far, despite a tremendous amount of scientific research and documentation, the FDA has not accepted the filing of the Stevia GRAS petition.

If the petition is accepted, several of the U.S. food giants are waiting in the wings to exploit the marketing potential of this all-natural, low-calorie, sugar-free supersweetener. One rumor has it that a U.S.-based company which markets a competitive synthetic product is already purchasing Stevia fields in Southern Ontario. If this is true, the floodgates may be ready to open, based on the surge of public opinion and scientific evidence supporting Stevia.

CHAPTER SIX

The Safety of Stevia

In May of 1991, the U.S. FDA issued an import ban on Stevia Rebaudiana leaves and extract which effectively blocked sales of Stevia here in this country. However, in September 1995, the FDA issued a revision to the Stevia import alert. The revision states that Stevia leaves or extract of Stevia leaves or Stevioside are allowed for import only if they are explicitly labeled as a dietary supplement or for use as an ingredient of a dietary supplement. The revised alert specifically excludes Stevia from being imported as a sweetener or flavoring agent. However, if Stevia is imported as a food supplement, the FDA will not detain or confiscate it. The revised import alert defines Stevia and its extracts, as did the original alert, as unapproved food additives and not affirmed as GRAS, (generally recognized as safe) in the United States. The revision states that available toxicological information on Stevia is inadequate to demonstrate its safety as a food additive or to affirm its status as GRAS.

What does this tell us about the safety of Stevia? In my opinion, very little. It would seem that the current revised alert represents a compromise. On the one hand, it makes a concession to the natural food industry that Stevia will be allowed to be imported and sold as a food supplement, but on the other hand, it protects the vested interests of the artificial sweetener conglomerates and the sugar lobby in removing Stevia as a sweetening or flavoring agent. The facts of science seem to have played very little part in this decision and the realities of politics seem to have influenced it a great deal.

This brings us back to the question – is Stevia safe? For an answer to this question, we need to delve into both the scientific research that has been done on Stevia since 1887 and its usage record over the past two centuries by Indian tribes in Paraguay as well as its modern usage worldwide.

In terms of the traditional usage of Stevia Rebaudiana by the Guarani Indians, there is rather little documentation to tell us how extensively it was used as a sweetener or whether any medicinal properties were ascribed to it. As one researcher noted, "It is often difficult or impossible to document early uses of plants by indigenous peoples because their knowledge may not have been shared with outsiders, but more often the information was ignored by colonists and by the time an appreciation existed for such data, the indigenous culture, including the ethnobotany, was destroyed or fragmentary at best." We are therefore indebted to men like Bertoni, Gosling and Dieterich (See Chapter 2) for their early reporting of the usage of Stevia as a sweetener by the native tribes. This reporting also begs the question of Stevia's safety, since primitive people are much more in tune with their environment and in harmony with their food supply than those of us who rely on others to qualify the safety and nutritive benefits of our food. The traditional usage of Stevia by the Guarani Indians is therefor a strong argument in favor of Stevia's safety.

The usage record of Stevia and Steviosides in the past twenty years is a second major argument for Stevia's safety. (See Chapter 5). With the massive quantities of Stevia Extracts and Stevioside that is consumed each year, the safety record of Stevia has been nothing short of amazing. There have been no known cases of Stevia overdoses or toxicity to humans reported around the world during the past forty years. This absence of toxicity is admitted, even by Stevia's most skeptical critics.

Scientific research has verified that Stevia and Steviosides are non-toxic in controlled laboratory experiments which have focused on the short-term consequences of the ingestion of very large quantities of Stevia and on the long-term consequences of more moderate dietary amounts of Stevia. The first of these studies was performed in 1931 by Pomeret and Lavielle.

This early study found Stevioside to be non-toxic to the rabbit, guinea pig and fowl and to be excreted without significant modification.

The first modern testing of Stevia's safety was performed in 1975 by Haruo Akashi and his associate, Dr. Yoko Yama, under the sponsorship of the Tama Biochemical Co. of Japan. This testing was divided into three separate studies: reproductive effects, short-term effects, and long-term effects. Their reproductive study concluded that there were no abnormalities or statistical differences in pregnancy rate among animals tested for the effects of Stevia administration. In terms of acute toxicity (short-term), they noted that "the safety of the three extracts (of Stevia) is estimated to be high." Their long-term toxicity results noted: "As a whole, administration of the maximum dose of 5g/Kg/day produced no adverse effects on the test animals." In other words, Stevia was found to be safe in both short-term and long-term toxicity studies.

These results have been confirmed in a number of other research studies conducted in Japan, Korea and the United States. From the Korean study, conducted at the University of Seoul, it was concluded that "No abnormalities in the growth rates of the animal groups treated with large amounts of Stevia Extract orally for 56 days could be observed. . . . From the experimental results, it can be postulated that Stevia Extract as well as Stevioside did not exhibit any acute or subacute toxicities to albino rats."

Another major Japanese study (Yamada, 1984) corroborated these results, concluding "when male and female rats were fed Stevia Extracts up to 1% of their feed for about two years, no significant dose-related changes were found in strength, general appearance, hematological and blood biochemic findings, organ weights, or macroscopic or microscopic findings."

A University of Illinois Research team confirmed Stevioside's short-term safety, along with Rebaudiosides A-C, Steviolbioside, and Dulcoside A, which are other biochemical constituents of Stevia, in a two-week experiment in which separate 2 g/Kg doses of each of these substances was administered to mice. (Medon, et al., 1982).

From a scientific perspective, then, as well as an historical and a modern usage perspective, it is clear that Stevia is a safe, non-toxic substance in both the short and long-term. However, there is one additional safety check which has been the source of Stevia's controversial recent history: the potential mutagenicity of Stevia's metabolites.

Mutagenicity testing is used primarily to determine whether a substance is a carcinogen (cancer-promoting substance) or not. It typically involves the use of live bacteria, like that which inhabits the human digestive tract, and the application of a test substance together with various activating substances to determine how this "stew" will effect the bacterial growth. Depending on the number of abnormal or mutated bacterial cells, a substance is labelled mutagenic (a potential carcinogen) or non-mutagenic (safe). A pertinent case in point is the synthetic sweetener Saccharin which was found to be mutagenic in a 1977 study and was temporarily banned by the FDA. Today it requires special labelling which warns consumers of the potential risks associated with using the product.

The first test of Stevia's mutagenic potential was conducted by the Food and Drug Safety Center of Japan at the request of the Stevia Association in 1979. An extract of dried Stevia leaves and a refined Stevioside preparation were tested using four strains of bacteria. The test revealed "no induction of mutation on all direct and metabolic activity." A second study of the potential mutagenicity of Stevia was conducted, once again by the Biological Safety Center of the National Institute of Hygienic Sciences in Tokyo, in 1983. A total of 190 synthetic and 52 natural food additives were evaluated, including an 85% Stevioside Extract. In this test, six strains of bacteria were evaluated for mutation. At a 12 mg/ml dose level, the Stevia Extract proved to be as mutagenically safe as chlorophyll or vanilla extract.

The Stevia controversy began in 1984 with the publication of research, performed by John Pezzuto and associates from the College of Pharmacy at the University of Illinois, Chicago. This research presented evidence that a metabolite of Stevioside, called Steviol, is mutagenic in the presence of two metabolic activating substances. This test was performed against a specific Salmonella strain of bacteria and used the metabolite Steviol rather than Stevioside or Stevia extracts. Two additional papers by the same team, published in 1985 and 1986, further advanced this proposition and presented evidence that another Stevioside metabolite was also potentially mutagenic since it is closely related to a known mutagen. On the strength of this research, the FDA initiated its import alert for Stevia, effectively shutting down sales in this country.

What is the strength of this research? Since I am not a scientist, it is not my place to evaluate the methods or conclusions of this study. However I can note the suppositions upon which it was built, as well as the reactions of other scientists and the rest of the world.

The key suppositions upon which the University of Illinois studies were built are as follows:

1. That the study itself was valid in the methodology followed and the materials used.
2. That no impurity or extraneous material might have modified the test results.
3. That Stevioside is broken down to Steviol in the human digestive tract in the same way that it is broken down in a rat's digestive tract.
4. That the Steviol is absorbed in part or in whole through normal digestive processes.
5. That the Steviol would come into direct contact with the metabolic activating agent which is contained in the microsomal portion of the liver.
6. That the Steviol is not converted to other innocuous metabolites or glycosides.

While I would not attempt to challenge the first supposition myself, a research team in England has made this challenge. In a short communication received in August of 1990, researchers from the Cell Mutation Unit at the University of Sussex in Brighton have noted a procedural fallacy in the University of Illinois studies. This fallacy involves the counting of mutagenic bacteria, before and after the test substances are applied, and the formula used to calculate the percentage increase of mutations. According to these researchers and earlier research cited, the formula used in the University of Illinois study could also demonstrate "that distilled water is mutagenic." Using a corrected formula, these researchers eliminated the possible mutagenicity of the Steviol metabolic mentioned earlier while leaving Steviol itself in an indeterminate status. Their conclusion mentions another inconsistency related to the saturation point of Steviol in solution and suggests "that it might be worth exploring the possibility that the (supposed) mutagenicity of Steviol . . . is due to an impurity."

The suggestion of an impurity is worth considering since the derivation of pure Steviol involves a number of steps including the application of L-butanol, sodium periodate and sodium hydroxide, silica gel, and a chloroform–methanol mixture.

The third supposition is also questionable since earlier experiments had shown that Stevioside was broken down into Steviol in the rat cecum. As noted by Bakal and Nabors, however, it is likely that the microflora of the human digestive tract is different from the cecal microflora of rats. Consequently, human metabolism of Stevioside into Steviol remains questionable, at best.

This same information also calls the fourth supposition into question.

The fifth supposition is an interesting one. It was stated by Pezzuto that Steviol is only mutagenic in the presence of a metabolic activating agent which is derived from the microsomal portion of a rat's liver. Assuming that human digestive breakdown might bring some Steviol into the liver, how could it be thus activated? The answer is that it must cross the intact cell walls of the liver in order to reach the microsomal fraction. And at least two studies have indicated that Stevioside and its metabolites are largely unable to do this. As a 1986 Brazilian study commented, "It seems that Stevioside . . . is not able to affect the adenine nucleotide carrier of the mitocondrial membrane in the intact cell because it does not permeate the plasma membrane."

The sixth and seventh presuppositions were noted by Pezzuto himself in qualifying the results of his experiments. That the body has self-protective mechanisms to convert or detoxify harmful substances is unquestionable. Whether these substances are necessary in the case of Stevia is the biggest question. Pezzuto apparently tested the effects of two substances, epoxide hydrolase and glutathione-s-epoxide-transferase in reducing Steviol's reported toxigenicity. Both were found ineffective when administered to mice. The larger issue, which he does not take up, is why no protective mechanism was activated in any of the experiments where test animals were fed Stevia, Stevia Extracts or Steviosides as a large part of their diet.

My conclusion, based upon the best information available, is that no protective mechanism was activated because none was needed. In short, Stevia has been shown to be a safe, natural product.

If scientific consensus means anything, the rest of the world agrees. Despite the Stevia "controversy," Stevia remains on the market in virtually every other country in the world. Only the U.S. FDA temporarily removed it. And today, it is available in the U.S. again, albeit on a qualified basis.

In conclusion, I would like to quote the remarks of two Japanese researchers involved in the testing of Stevia for many years:

> *The present authors have tasted Stevia sweeteners in our daily works for many years and felt no abnormality on their health. . . . The reported safety studies on Stevia as mentioned above and over a hundred years use by native inhabitants in Paraguay may prove that Stevia sweeteners are highly safe and sufficiently feasible for use in food.*

CHAPTER SEVEN

How to Use Stevia

S tevia's usage is traditionally and primarily as a sweetener. However, it is also being used as a medicine, a cosmetic ingredient, a pickling agent and a dentrifice. Here are a few of the tips and suggestions I have picked up from Stevia experts and enthusiasts across the country:

1. Stevia has traditionally been used to sweeten teas and coffee-like beverages. It can also replace sugar or honey in most other beverages as well.
2. Stevia does not break down when it is heated, so it can be used in foods that are baked or cooked.
3. Stevia is a "flavor enhancer" as well as a sweetener. It helps to bring out the true flavors in cereals, breads, juices, berries, sherbets, candies, yogurt, ice cream, chewing gum, pickles, toothpaste and mouthwash in addition to its normal sweetening activity.
4. Stevia can be used topically as a masque ingredient. The following "recipe" was submitted by Victoria and Robert Stitzer of Fort Lauderdale, FL:

Mix together 1 tsp. Redmond or Green Clay, ½ tsp. Green Stevia, 1 tsp. water. Add more water if needed. Apply on clean face and neck. Let dry for 10–15 minutes—not longer! Loosen the masque with warm wet cloth, then remove it and splash the skin at least 10 times. Blot it dry and apply favorite moisturizer.

This masque is cleansing, healing, rejuvenating and anti-inflammatory. It literally pulls out impurities. For a more serious skin condition I add contents of one capsule of Goldenseal Root to the above mixture.

5. The Stitzers also recommend Stevia as a remedy for bleeding gums and as a gargle for sore throats and cold sores. This makes sense because of Stevia's mild anti-bacterial activity. Here are their comments:

I used to suffer from bleeding gums a long time ago and someone recommended I try the following recipe. In 2 days I was astonished by the results.

Sprinkle some white concentrated powdered Stevia on your toothbrush, apply toothpaste over it and brush, gently massaging the gums by making circular motions.

Also, try to gargle with Stevia (½ glass warm water with ¼ tsp. Stevia) to alleviate conditions like sore throat, mouth sores, painful gums. It always works for both of us. Try it. If it doesn't help, at least, you know it won't hurt.

6. Because Stevia has been shown to inhibit the development of plaque and cavities, it is a natural for toothpastes, powders and gels. (See recipe in Chapter 8.)
7. While Stevia is being touted in Brazil as an anti-diabetic agent, the research on Stevia's effect on blood sugar metabolism is far from conclusive. Consequently, I do not recommend or endorse this application at the present time.

CHAPTER EIGHT

Growing Your Own Stevia

I f you enjoy gardening, Stevia can be a rewarding herb to grow. While it's not feasible for most of us to grow sugarcane or sorghum in our backyard, several Stevia plants will fit nicely into a small garden. Recipes utilizing Green Stevia Powder are now available, and the whole leaves add to the flavor of herbal teas.

Stevia rebaudiana is a tender perennial, native to semi-humid subtropical regions of Paraguay and Brazil. Wild plants occur on acid soils that are constantly moist, but not inundated, often near the edge of marshes or streams where the soil is sandy (Brandle et al., 1998). In the garden, too, Stevia doesn't like to dry out, but standing water will encourage rot and disease. Stevia can be a successful garden plant in most climates with the use of a few simple techniques. Raised beds or hills prevent "wet feet," while an organic mulch and frequent watering ensure a constant supply of moisture.

In North America, Stevia survives winters only in the warmest areas such as southern California, Florida, and Mexico. Research in Japan indicates a critical winter soil temperature of 32°F to 35°F (Sumida, 1980). Stevia is a weak perennial, so plants grown as perennials should be replaced every few years. In colder areas, Stevia is planted after the last frost and treated as an annual. Longer summer days found at higher latitudes favor leaf yield and Stevioside content (Shock, 1982).

Soil Preparation

While tolerant of most soil types, Stevia prefers a sandy loam or loam. Any well-drained soil that produces a good crop of vegetables should work fine. Incorporating organic matter is the best way to improve heavy, high-clay soils. A rich compost made with leaves, grass, hay, kitchen waste, manure, and other organic residues will improve soil structure and supply nutrients. Finished compost may be tilled, disked, or spaded into the soil before planting or used as a mulch later on. A "green manure" crop the previous year such as oats, rye, or legumes will also improve heavy soils. Stevia occurs naturally on soils of pH 4 to 5, but thrives with soil pH as high as 7.5. However, Stevia does not tolerate saline soils (Shock, 1982).

While a good compost usually satisfies nutrient requirements, soil testing or plant symptoms may alert you to deficiencies. Mark Langan of *Mulberry Creek HerbFarm* recommends low nitrogen or organic fertilizers. Excess nitrogen promotes rank growth with poor flavor. Bone meal, blood meal, cottonseed meal, guano, or dried manure provide nitrogen that is released slowly. Rock phosphate or bone meal provide phosphorous. Greensand is a good source of potassium. Rock phosphate, bone meal, and greensand offer a wide range of trace minerals. For maximum nutrient availability, work organic fertilizers into the soil a few months before planting, or mix with compost. For poor fertility soils, Blas Oddone (1997) of *Guarani Botanicals, Inc.* recommends incorporating 6 to 7 pounds of cattle manure per square yard. When using chemical fertilizers, a low nitrogen formula such as 6-24-24 is recommended in a split application – at planting time and again in mid summer. (Columbus, 1997). Steve Marsden of *Herbal Advantage, Inc.* simply uses a balanced vegetable fertilizer at the dose and intervals recommended on the container for vegetables.

Unless your soil is very sandy, raised beds are ideal for Stevia. A raised growing surface prevents standing water and reduces compaction. Beds should be 3 to 4 feet wide and 4 to 6 inches high. Till, disk, or spade the whole area thoroughly, then mark bed boundaries with string or garden hoses. Dig soil from the paths, 1 to 3 feet wide, and toss onto the beds until they reach the desired height. Beds may be left in place permanently. By walking only on paths, soil compaction is reduced. A mulch such as newspapers, grass clippings, or landscape fabric on paths will help control weeds. While not necessary, sides on the beds can be attractive and functional. Concrete blocks may be used, or rot-resistant wood such as cedar, redwood, or locust. Raised bed "kits" made from plastic are available as well. Treated wood should be avoided because of possible soil contamination.

Mr. Marsden prefers the "hill" method commonly used for sweet corn. Set plants in low hills spaced 12 to 18 inches apart. Periodically during the growing season, pull more soil up around the plants with a hoe. This will tend to smother weeds and drain away surface water that could encourage disease.

Getting Started

Stevia rebaudiana seeds are rarely available because of production problems and poor germination, so plants are generally used instead. Plants are available from several mail order sources (see Appendix I). Be sure you are getting *Stevia rebaudiana* (*Stevia* is the genus and *rebaudiana* is the species) since this is the only sweet variety. Stevia stems are brittle, but nurseries have developed packing methods to protect them in transit. Arrange for plants to arrive soon after your last frost date. Later on, high temperatures may stress transplants. Transfer plants to the garden as soon as possible after arrival, making sure they don't dry out in the meantime.

In garden beds, space plants 10 to 12 inches apart in each row, with two rows per bed. Stagger rows so that plants end up in a zigzag pattern. Use a trowel to dig a hole, then pour in some water and set the plants a bit deeper than they were in the pot, so the root ball is covered by a thin layer of garden soil. After back-filling around the roots, water again to settle the soil. If the weather is hot and sunny at planting time, it's a good idea to place a thin mulch around the plants to reduce moisture loss. Cool night temperatures will halt plant growth. For early plantings or areas with cool summers, hotcaps or row covers will allow faster growth and offer protection from late frosts. Don't let the plants overheat on hot days, however.

If you are fortunate enough to obtain high-quality Stevia seeds, they are easily germinated indoors under lights. Seedlings grow slowly, so allow 7 to 8 weeks from seed to transplanting (Columbus, 1997). Only black or dark brown seeds are viable. A tan or clear color suggests they are empty shells, lacking an embryo. You can verify this by slicing some seeds in half. Good seeds will be solid and white inside. Even firm, black seeds tend to lose viability rapidly. A germination test will indicate what percentage of the seeds are likely to sprout. Place 10 or more seeds on a wet paper towel. Fold the towel in half 3 times, then slip it into a plastic bag kept at 72°F to 80°F. Count sprouted seeds after 7 days and divide by the total number of seeds you were testing, then multiply by 100 to get the germination percentage.

A plastic flat covered by a clear plastic dome, available from garden retailers, makes an ideal germination chamber when placed beneath a growing light. Place a thermometer inside and maintain a 70°F to 75°F temperature by adjusting the level of the light. Use small containers (with drainage holes) or plastic cell packs filled with standard potting soil. Place 3 or 4 seeds on the soil surface in each container and cover with a thin layer (about 1/8 inch) of horticultural vermiculite. Water from below as needed by pouring water into the tray. Seedlings should emerge in 1 to 2 weeks. Thin to one plant per container. Extra seedlings may be transplanted to empty containers.

Plant Care

In general, Stevia should be treated as a vegetable crop. When hot weather sets in, usually a month after planting, beds should be mulched 3 to 6 inches deep with organic residue such as grass clippings, chopped leaves, straw, hay, or compost. This will protect the shallow feeder roots and hold in moisture. Plant growth is slow at first, accelerating by mid summer.

A consistent moisture supply is important for Stevia. Irrigate once or twice a week, whenever rain fails to water the plants. Sandy soils require more frequent irrigation. Trickle irrigation is ideal, ensuring consistent moisture levels without wetting leaves. A simple and effective system is the black, "weeping" soaker hose made from recycled rubber. Place a soaker hose between the two rows of plants, beneath the mulch. Attach to a garden hose and turn the water on at a trickle for a couple of hours. The system can be automated with the addition of a timer.

Side-dressing is usually not necessary, but low nitrogen or organic fertilizer may be applied in the summer as plant growth begins to accelerate. Excess nitrogen causes tender growth and reduced leaf sweetness. Mr. Oddone recommends application of a 10-10-12 foliar fertilizer directly on leaves at 30 and 60 days from transplanting.

Stevia stems are prone to breakage during high winds. Mr. Langan advises pinching tips out every 3 to 4 weeks for the first month to encourage side branching, resulting in a bushier plant. Grow in a protected area if possible. Supporting the plants with a "corral" made from strings tied to stakes is another strategy.

Stevia may be affected by two lesion-producing fungal diseases, *Septoria steviae* and *Sclerotinia sclerotiorum* (Brandle et al., 1998). With Sclerotinia, dark brown lesions form on stems, near the soil line, followed by wilting and eventual collapse of the plant. Stevia plants are usually full grown before diseases appear. As harvest time nears, commercial growers watch plants closely and harvest the entire crop at the first sign of disease. Meticulous weed control (by hand) permits strong growth, which helps plants resist disease. Humid, wet weather and standing water favor the development of fungal diseases, making raised beds or hills a preventative measure. Additionally, avoid wetting leaves during irrigation. Stevia is usually the last plant insects will feed on, so pests are seldom a problem outdoors. Aphids, thrips, and whiteflies can cause damage in heavily infested greenhouses.

Harvesting

Use fresh leaves for tea or eat a few right off the plant. They taste great with mint leaves. Sweetness (Stevioside content) is greatest just before flowering, which is triggered by short day lengths (Brandle et al., 1998). The onset of blossoming ranges from mid summer to late fall. Plants should be harvested before the first frost or as soon as blossoming begins, whichever comes first. Cut entire plants just above ground level. When growing Stevia as a perennial or for early harvests, clip the plants 6 inches from the ground so they will survive and re-grow (Shock, 1982). Harvest in the morning, after dew has evaporated.

Plants are easily dried by hanging upside down in a dry, warm, drafty location. Bunch a few plants together and bind at the stem end with a rubber band, then slip a paper clip bent into an "S" shape under the rubber band. Hang by the other end of the paperclip. If you have lots of plants, hang them from strings or wires strung across the ceiling. After a few days, rake leaves from the stems with your fingers and gather for storage in a clean container such as a glass jar. They keep well for years. Stems are less sweet, so toss them on the compost pile. An alternative method is to strip fresh leaves from stems and spread on elevated screens in the sunshine, on a day with low relative humidity (less than 60%). If drying takes 8 hours or less, according to Steve Marsden, very little Stevioside will be lost. A food dehydrator on low heat (100°F to 110°F) will do an excellent job as well. Leaves are crisp, crumbly, and bright green when fully dry.

While whole leaves are great for making tea, it's easy to turn them into Green Stevia Powder with a kitchen blender, food processor, or coffee grinder with metal blades. With the blender bowl half full, process dry leaves at high speed for a few seconds. Collect the fine powder for use in recipes calling for Green Stevia Powder. Use a clean glass jar for long-term storage.

Propagation and Container Growing

Stevia stem cuttings root easily without hormones, but only under long day conditions. A fluorescent shop or plant growth light both work well. Leave the light on 14 to 16 hours per day, 5 to 9 inches above the cuttings. An automatic timer will make the job easier. Even with artificial light, Stevia cuttings root most easily during the long days of spring. Cuttings should be taken in March for transplanting in May or June. Plants from later cuttings may be over-wintered in pots under fluorescent lights.

Fall cuttings root successfully with the use of rooting hormones. Use a low-strength rooting compound available from garden retailers or make your own natural compound with Steve Marsden's recipe. Harvest a handful of willow branch tips and remove the foliage, then liquefy in a blender with twice the volume of water. Dip cuttings in this mixture before placing in the rooting medium.

Coarse or medium grade horticultural vermiculite works well for rooting Stevia. Mr. Marsden prefers a peat-lite mix that includes bark, especially for outdoor propagation beds. Coarse, clean sand may be used as well. Place small pots, or cell packs with drainage holes, in flats or trays to facilitate watering from below as needed. With a sharp blade or pruning tool, make cuttings 2 to 4 inches long. Each cutting should have 2 or 3 nodes. A node is where leaves attach to the stem. Cut between, rather than at the nodes. (Sumida, 1980). Plunge the proximal end (closest to the roots on the mother plant) of the cutting into the rooting medium far enough so that at least one node is buried and at least one node remains above the surface. Remove all leaves from buried nodes. Above the surface, remove large leaves by cutting or pinching leaf stems, taking care not to damage the tiny axillary leaves emerging behind large leaves. These axillary leaves are the growing points of your new plant. Keep cuttings at 60∞F to 70∞F. Indoors, under lights, misting is not necessary. Outdoors, or in a sunlit greenhouse, cuttings should be misted several times per day until roots are well formed. After about a week, growth should be evident if rooting was successful. After 3 to 4 weeks, transfer plants to larger pots (at least 3-4 inches in diameter) with standard potting soil. Transplant these to the garden in another 2 to 4 weeks or keep as a container plant.

For older plants, keep the fluorescent light a few inches above the foliage. When stems reach 7 to 10 inches in length, cut them back to promote branching and vigor. Over-wintered plants look devitalized by the end of the winter, but regain vigor when transplanted outdoors. Some plants will inevitably be lost, so grow more than you think you'll need. Stevia may also be grown outdoors in containers such as gallon pots. If you start with a high-quality potting soil that has organic fertilizers mixed in, further fertilization may be unnecessary, but a monthly watering with a dilute seaweed solution can be beneficial. Mr. Langan recommends a balanced, slow release fertilizer applied every two weeks for container plants. He also advises using wooden containers or the double pot method to insulate roots from summer heat. Place in full sun when it's cool, but provide shade during hot weather, making sure the soil doesn't dry out. For perennial production, bring containers indoors before the first frost.

CHAPTER NINE

Recipes—Now We're Cookin!

---- ❦ ----

Carob Chip Cake

2½ cups whole wheat flour

2 tablespoons green STEVIA powder

1½ teaspoons baking powder (aluminum-free)

1¼ teaspoons baking soda

⅓ cup oil

1 egg, lightly beaten

1 teaspoon vanilla

1–2 cups carob chips

1–2 cups natural applesauce (may need more to make cake batter consistency)

1–2 teaspoons cinnamon

Preheat oven to 325°. Mix all ingredients together. Put into a 13" by 9" pan. Bake for 30–40 minutes.

Tahini Energy Balls

¾ cup tahini
¼ cup water
1 cup ground sunflower or pumpkin seeds (or mixture of
  both)
½ cup powdered milk or soymilk
⅛–¼ teaspoon STEVIA extract powder
½ cup dried soybeans
½ cup carob chips
peppermint oil if desired, 2–4 drops

Mix ingredients. Refrigerate about 45 minutes. Make into balls. Keep re-
frigerated until ready to serve. Makes 2–3 dozen.

Pumpkin Cookies

5 cups whole wheat flour
2 teaspoons baking powder
3 teaspoons pumpkin pie spice
5 teaspoons green STEVIA powder
4 eggs, lightly beaten
1 cup applesauce
1 can pumpkin
1½–2 teaspoons cinnamon
½ teaspoon ground cloves
2 teaspoons vanilla
May want to use extra milk, cinnamon, pumpkin pie spice.

Preheat oven to 325°. Mix ingredients. Place on greased cookie sheets and
bake for 11 minutes. Makes 8 dozen.

Cranberry Tea Bread

2 cups whole wheat flour
2 teaspoons baking powder
½ teaspoon salt (optional)
3 tablespoons oil
¼ cup unsweetened carob chips (optional)
1½ tablespoons grated orange zest
2 cups fresh cranberries
1 egg
2–3 teaspoons green STEVIA powder

Preheat oven to 350°. Grease & flour a 2 qt. loaf pan. Mix flour, baking powder, stevia & salt. Mix in oil until it looks like coarse bread crumbs. Add carob chips, orange zest & cranberries. Stir to coat with the flour mixture. Stir in egg. Mix well. Spoon into pan (batter will be stiff). Bake 1 hour or until done.

Banana Bread

2 cups whole wheat flour (for wheat allergies substitute
    2 cups soy, rice or flour of your choice)
1 teaspoon baking powder
2 teaspoons green STEVIA powder
2 eggs
1 cup applesauce or oil
¼ cup buttermilk (may need more)
1–6 mashed bananas

Preheat oven to 325°. Mix dry ingredients together, then mix in the rest. Add a couple handfulls of nuts (& raisins) if you like. Pour into a greased and floured loaf pan and bake 45 minutes to an hour.

Pumpkin Cake

2 cups whole wheat flour
2 teaspoon baking powder
2–3 teaspoons green STEVIA powder
2 teaspoons cinnamon
1 cup applesauce
1 cup milk
4 eggs
1 small pumpkin
1 cup chopped nuts (may also add raisins, taste great in here)

Empty pumpkin, slice into sections and steam until tender—then mash or puree in a blender. Stew pumpkin down until it becomes a thick paste.

Preheat oven to 350°. Mix dry ingredients. Add wet ones and mix well. Pour into a greased and floured 13" by 9" pan. Bake for 40 minutes or until done.

Vanilla Icing

2 8–oz. neufchatel cheese
2 inches of ground vanilla bean
½–¾ teaspoon STEVIA extract powder
2–3 tablespoons Ghee
May add a little milk or water to get the right consistency.

Mix these all well and spread on your dessert or pastry. Tastes great on the cake above.

—— ❧ ——

Baked Fruit Dessert

2 cups each fresh (or frozen) peaches, blueberries, strawberries
   (or whatever fruits you choose)
2 tablespoons arrowroot powder
1 teaspoon green stevia powder

Mix these all together in a bowl and pour into a greased 13" by 9" pan.

Topping:
1½ cups oat flour (or flour of your choice)
2 teaspoons baking powder
1 teaspoon green STEVIA powder
3 tablespoons applesauce
1 egg, beaten
½ cup milk
(can use 2–3 tablespoons of Ghee)

Mix these well. Sprinkle over the top of the fruit and bake for 20–25 minutes in a 375° oven.

—— ❧ ——

Oatmeal Apple Muffins

1 cup whole wheat flour
1 cup rolled oats
½ teaspoon salt
3 teaspoons baking powder
½ teaspoon nutmeg
2 teaspoons cinnamon
1½ teaspoons green STEVIA powder

1 egg
¾ cup milk
¼ cup oil (or ¼ cup applesauce)
1 medium apple, cored and course-chopped
¾ cup raisins

Preheat oven to 400°. Mix first seven ingredients thoroughly. In separate bowl, mix remaining ingredients. Gradually mix dry ingredients into moist ingredients. Spoon into greased muffin tins. Bake 15 to 20 minutes.

Carob Brownies

⅔ cup whole wheat flour
2 tablespoons carob powder
1½ teaspoon baking powder
1½ teaspoons green STEVIA powder
¼ teaspoon salt
⅓ cup oil (or ⅓ cup applesauce)
⅓ cup water
2 eggs, lightly beaten
1 tablespoon vanilla
½ cup grated coconut (unsweetened)
½ cup nuts (your choice)
½ cup carob chips (unsweetened)

Preheat oven to 325 degrees. Thoroughly mix together first five ingredients. Add oil, water, eggs, and vanilla. Mix well. Add remaining ingredients. Stir well until mixed. Pour into greased 8" by 8" pan. Bake 20 minutes or until toothpick inserted slightly off-center comes out clean.

Whole Grain Soda Bread (no yeast)

1½ cups whole wheat flour
1 cup rolled oats
1½ cups oat flour
1½ teaspoons green STEVIA powder
1 tablespoon baking powder
1 tablespoon baking soda
1½ teaspoons salt
6 tablespoons butter (or 1 tablespoons margarine or
   applesauce)
1½ cups raisins
1 teaspoon caraway seeds
1½ cups buttermilk

Preheat oven 350 degrees Mix first seven ingredients thoroughly in large bowl. Cut butter or margarine into flour mixture to form coarse crumbs. Stir in raisins and caraway seeds. Add buttermilk (dough will be sticky). Turn dough out onto well floured surface. Kneed for 8 to 10 strokes until thoroughly mixed. Shape into ball and place on greased pizza pan. Lightly dust top with flour. In center, cut an X about ¼" deep. Bake one hour, and let cool on wire rack.

Recipes by Vicki Mosser

Peanut Butter Bars

1 cup natural peanut butter
1 cup finely ground pecans
2 eggs
1 cup rolled oats
1 cup whole wheat flour
4 drops of clear liquid STEVIA

Mix these ingredients and press into two 8" x 8" baking pans. The mixture will be crumbly. Bake as 350 degrees for ten minutes. Remove from oven and spread the following mixture on them.

1 cup milk
¾ cup natural peanut butter
2 egg yolks
2 tablespoons flour
4 drops of clear liquid STEVIA

Beat this mixture until smooth.

Beat until stiff:
2 egg whites
1 teaspoon baking power

Fold the egg whites into the first five ingredients (after you have mixed them). Spread this mixture on the crust you removed from the oven and return to oven and bake for 15 to 20 minutes more. Do not cut until cool or it will skin the top layer back. Makes 24 bars.

Cabbage Pineapple Salad

4 cups of finely chopped cabbage
2 cups of finely chopped fresh pineapple

Dressing:
1 cup of yogurt
3 tablespoons lemon juice
4 drops of clear liquid STEVIA or ¼ teaspoon
    STEVIA extract powder

Mix all ingredients and chill. Serves 8.

Three Bean Salad

2 cups cooked and drained green beans cut into short pieces
2 cups cooked and drained wax beans cut into short pieces
2 cups of cooked and drained kidney beans
½ cup finely chopped onion

Dressing:
1 cup yogurt
3 tablespoons lemon juice
4 drops of clear liquid STEVIA or ¼ teaspoon of
    white STEVIA powder
½ teaspoon black or red pepper

Mix all ingredients and chill to marinate before serving. Serves 6.

Carob Cupcakes

1⅔ cups flour
½ cup carob powder
½ teaspoon baking powder
1 teaspoon baking soda
½ teaspoon salt
1½ teaspoons STEVIA extract powder
½ cup soft butter (or ½ cup applesauce)
2 eggs
½ cup water
½ cup carob chips (unsweetened)
½ cup chopped nuts (your choice)

Preheat oven to 400 degrees. Thoroughly mix first six ingredients in separate bowl. Mix remaining ingredients. Add dry ingredients to moist and mix well. Pour into greased and floured cupcake tins. Bake 15–20 minutes until toothpick inserted comes out clean.

Recipes by Janelle Myers

Jean's Wonder Pumpkin Pie with Stevia

Graham Cracker Crust

1½ cups graham crackers, fine-crushed or blended
⅛ teaspoon STEVIA extract powder
6 tablespoons melted butter
(1 teaspoon cinnamon)

Preheat oven to 300 degrees. Reserve ¼ to ½ of the crust. Put the rest into the pan to the desired thickness. Bake before filling for about 15 minutes. Cool before placing custard into shell.

continued

Pumpkin Custard

2 eggs beaten slightly
1¾ cup pumpkin or butternut squash
3 tablespoons sugar
¼ teaspoon STEVIA extract powder
½ teaspoon salt
1 teaspoon ground cinnamon
½ teaspoon ginger
¼ teaspoon ground cloves
1½ cups evaporated milk or 1½ cups water with
　　5 or 6 tablespoons dry milk

Preheat oven to 425 degrees. Pour pumpkin into shell and place the rest of the crust on top. Bake for 15 minutes. Reduce heat to 350 degrees for an additional 45 minutes or until knife inserted near center comes out clean. Cool. Garnish with whipped topping if desired.

Recipe from Andrea Health Foods, North Newton, KS.

Sesame Seed Candy

2 cups sesame seeds
½ cup coconut oil
½ teaspoon STEVIA extract (white powdered)
½ teaspoon vanilla
1 heaping tablespoon peanut butter
1 tablespoon carob

Start the blender with oil. Gradually, add in sesame seeds. Push seeds down and under the blades. Add Stevia and vanilla to the mixture and continue blending until smooth. Divide mixture into three bowls: add peanut butter to one, carob to the next, and leave one plain. Shape into balls. Makes approx. 1½ dozen candies.

Recipe by Life Extension Intl., Fort Lauderdale, FL

Fig Bars

2 cups black figs, soaked and minced
1 cup coconut, freshly grated or dried
¼ tsp. STEVIA extract (white powdered)
1 teaspoon vanilla extract

Combine all ingredients well, form into bars or any other shape. Refrigerate and enjoy! Yield: approx. 1 dozen bars.

Variation: add 1 cup of nut meal, or coarsely chopped nuts in place of the coconut, and use coconut to dust the bars.

Raw Tomato/Herb Soup (Hot or Chilled)

Puree in a blender or processor *(I use VitaMix so that the soup comes out hot)*

10–12 raw plum tomatoes, skinned (canned may also be used)
½ cup fresh herbs, minced (choose one kind: basil, dill, parsley or cilantro)
¼ teaspoon STEVIA extract (white powdered)
1–2 tablespoons olive oil
2 tablespoons balsamic vinegar
1–2 tablespoons tamari or soy sauce

Hot soup can be served with white or brown rice or as is garnished with a sprig of fresh herb.

If chilled—garnish with fresh herbs, cayenne and chopped walnuts or pecans (optional). *Unmistakably delicious!*

Recipes by Life Extension Intl., Fort Lauderdale, FL.

❦

Eggless Mayonnaise

1 cup almond milk or unflavored soy milk
1 tablespoons onion powder
1 tablespoons sea salt or salt substitute
¼–⅓ teaspoon STEVIA extract (white powdered)
juice of 1 fresh lemon
2 cups of cold pressed oil (safflower, canola, etc.)

Put "milk" in food processor fitted with the metal blade and add onion powder, salt, Stevia and Lemon juice. Process for about 30 seconds as you slowly add the oil through the feed tube. The mixture will begin to thicken. Longer processing will result in thicker mayonnaise. Makes 3 cups.
This mayonnaise has very few calories and no cholesterol.

❦

Frozen Dessert "Strawberry Granita"

½ cup very hot (not boiling!) water
¼ teaspoon STEVIA extract (white powdered)
1 cup coarse-cracked ice cubes
2 pints strawberries, stemmed, rinsed and quartered
1 tablespoon fresh lime juice (or more to taste)
sliced fresh strawberries

Combine hot water and Stevia in blender and process until Stevia is dissolved. Add ice and blend until mixture is slushy. With blender running, gradually add strawberries and process until berries are pureed. Add lime juice. Taste and add more lime juice, if needed.

Place mixture in 13" x 9" baking pan and freeze, using fork to stir slushy center into almost frozen edges every 20 minutes or so, until mixture is semi-frozen, about 1½ hours. To serve, scoop granita into dessert bowls or wine glasses. Garnish with sliced strawberries. Makes about 6 servings.

Home-Pickled Vegetables

Pickling Juice:

1 cup apple cider vinegar

1 cup water

¼ teaspoon STEVIA extract (white powdered)

6 sprigs fresh dill

½ teaspoon dried red chili flakes

3 cloves garlic, peeled

2 cinnamon sticks

3 bay leaves

1 teaspoon ground turmeric

1 teaspoon whole mustard seeds

2 teaspoons kosher salt

Mixed Vegetables:

1 cup cauliflower florets

1 medium onion, sliced

2 carrots, peeled and sliced

¼ head sliced green cabbage

2 medium zucchini, sliced

2 small yellow squash (½ cup)

1 medium red bell pepper, julienned

1 medium green bell pepper, julienned

1 medium cucumber, sliced

To make juice:

In a nonreactive saucepan, bring all ingredients (except Stevia) to a boil over high heat. Reduce heat and simmer 10 minutes. Remove from heat. In about 1 minute stir in Stevia until dissolved.

continued

To make vegetables:

Place all the vegetables in a nonreactive bowl. Pour the hot juice over the veggies. Place a plate with a smaller diameter than the bowl atop the veggies and top with a weight (a heavy object) so that the veggies are submerged. Let sit at room temperature for 3 hours. Cover or transfer to jars and refrigerate overnight. Makes 5 cups. Will keep up to 2 weeks.

Recipes by Life Extension Intl., Fort Lauderdale, FL

Tropical Stevia–Green Smoothie

2 cups pineapple juice
1 banana
1 large kiwi, peeled
1 tablespoon barley grass or spirulina powder
½–1 teaspoon green STEVIA powder

Blend all ingredients together in electric blender.

Note: The green powders are especially compatible with the Kiwi and Pineapple.

Recipe by Karl Mincin, Consulting Nutritionist,
Nutrition Consulting Center, Concrete, WA

Stevia Ambrosia

1 quart organic aloe juice
1 quart peppermint or spearmint tea
juice of one large or two small lemons
1 clove of finely minced garlic
1 tablespoon bee pollen, propolis and royal jelly powder or
    extract (available from YS Royal Jelly and Honey Farms)
STEVIA powder or extract (to taste)

Combine ingredients in a large beverage container. Pau D'Arco tea may be added, as desired, to increase the health benefits. This is an excellent cleansing/healing/detoxifying beverage. Garnish with peppermint leaves or lemon slices.

Nature's Own Tooth Powder

½ oz. peelu powder
1 oz. baking soda (aluminum free)
½ oz. propolis powder
½ oz. green STEVIA powder (or equivalent amount of
    powdered extract)

Shake in a small bottle and you are ready to brush.
The mixture can be made into a paste through stirring into several ounces of vegetable glycerine and flavored with peppermint oil or powder.
Myrrh Oil may be added to increase the astringent and bacteriocidal properties of the paste.

Recipes by David Richard

Monster Cookie Balls

2 cups rolled oats
1 large apple, finely diced
¾ cup of raisins or currants
1 cup of nut butter (your choice)
¼–½ pound whole pecans
½ stick of butter or non-hydrogenated margarine
½ cup carob chips (optional)
2 whole eggs
1 cup of spring or filtered water
2 teaspoons green STEVIA powder or ½ teaspoon
  STEVIA extract powder

Combine rolled oats, eggs, water and butter in a mixing bowl. Stir in nut butter and remaining ingredients (except the pecans). Form into balls and place onto an oiled cookie sheet. Place a whole pecan on top of each ball. Bake at 350 degrees for 10–12 minutes.

Recipe by David Richard

Sugar-Free Hot Cocoa

	1 Cup	*Family*
Milk	1 cup	4 cups
Pure cocoa or instant carob powder	1 tablespoon	⅓ cup
STEVIA Extract Powder	pinch	pinches!
Malted milk (optional)	1 teaspoon	1 tablespoon

Slowly heat milk on stove. (Do not boil!) After hot, mix in powders and stir until smooth. Add a very small amount of Stevia until desired sweetness is attained. A small amount of Sucanat can be added, as desired, for a more sugary taste.

Recipe by Dan Richard

Stevia-Sweet Chocolate Chip Cookies

1 stick butter (½ cup)
¼ teaspoon STEVIA extract powder
1 tablespoon sucanat or honey (optional)
1 egg
½ teaspoon vanilla
½ cup unbleached wheat flour
½ cup whole wheat flour
½ teaspoon salt
½ teaspoon baking soda
1 cup rolled oats
¼ cup chopped nuts
½ cup chocolate chips or carob chips

Combine first 4 ingredients including softened butter. Mix together. Gradually add the following ingredients in order with slight variations possible. Divide into cookies and bake 10 minutes at 375 degrees. The texture will be different from conventional cookies, but, eaten warm, are quite delicious.

For a breakfast treat, eliminate the chocolate chips and add an equal amount of raisins.

The recipe listed reduces the sugar content 70% below traditional recipes.

Recipe by Dan Richard, Carol Stream, IL

———————— ❦ ————————

WHEAT-FREE • SUGAR-FREE • FAT-FREE
Honeyleaf Multigrain Muffins

Dry Ingredients:

1½ cup mixed wholegrain flour (½ cup each: barley, rice, spelt flour)

½ cup almond meal (can substitute other nut or seed meal or flour)

1 teaspoon baking soda

1 teaspoon baking powder

Wet Ingredients:

1 cup prune juice (can substitute apricot or pear)

¼ cup honey (can substitute rice or FOS syrup)

2 tablespoons oil (optional)

1 egg beaten

2 tablespoons green STEVIA ("Honeyleaf") powder (stir into wet ingredients)

Mix dry and wet ingredients separatley, then combine, mixing only enough to blend evenly; do not overstir. Spoon into oiled muffin tins. Bake 17 minutes in preheated 350 degree oven. Transfer to cooling rack. Makes 9 muffins.

Recipe by Karl Mincin, Consulting Nutritionist,
Nutrition Resource Center, Concrete, WA
(360) 853-7610

Winter's Edge Mulled Cider

1 orange
1 lemon
12 whole cloves
6 cups natural apple cider or juice
½ teaspoon STEVIA liquid extract
3 cinnamon sticks
12 whole allspice berries
⅓ cup natural honey (optional—may substitute rice or
    fruit syrup)

1) Using a skewer, pierce the orange and lemon. Insert cloves; slice fruit.
2) Combine citrus, cider, cinnamon, stevia and allspice in a saucepan. Bring
   to a simmer—do not boil. Simmer 5 minutes.
3) Pour cider through a fine mesh strainer into mugs. Discard fruit and
   seasonings. Garnish with cinnamon sticks and citrus strips.
Makes 6 cups.

Slice 'n Bake Stevia Cookies

½ pound butter
1 egg
½ cup molasses
3 cups whole wheat pastry flour
1 cup lecithin granules
1 teaspoon STEVIA extract powder
1 teaspoon sea salt
½ teaspoon baking soda (aluminum-free)
1 teaspoon natural vanilla extract
1 bottle natural fruit spread

continued

Whip butter. Add beaten egg and molasses – whip mixture. Sift dry ingredients together and stir in lecithin. Mix well with butter. Add vanilla. Make two rolls in wax paper. Chill 3–4 hours. Slice ½" and bake at 350 degrees for 8–12 minutes. The last minute or so, dab a small amount of natural fruit spread on each. Cool on wire rack. Yields 4 dozen.

Apple Pan Cake

½ stick and 3 tablespoons of butter, divided
½ teaspoon STEVIA extract powder
1 teaspoon ground cinnamon
½ teaspoon ground nutmeg
2 tart apples
2 teaspoons fresh lemon juice
1⅓ cups whole wheat pastry flour
½ cup honey (may substitute rice or fruit syrup)
1¾ teaspoons baking powder
¼ teaspoon sea salt
½ cup whole milk
½ cup water
1 teaspoon natural vanilla
1 egg, separated
½ cup chopped pecans

1) Preheat oven to 375 degrees. Melt ½ stick butter in 8" square baking pan. Add honey and spices; mix well.
2) Peel and core apples. Thinly slice into rings and arrange over honey. Sprinkle with lemon and set aside.
3) Combine flour, Stevia, baking powder and salt in a large bowl. Cut in remaining butter with a pastry blender until the mixture becomes course crumbs. Add milk, water and vanilla. Beat on low to moisten and, again, for two minutes on medium. Blend in yolk and pecans.

4) Whip egg whites to stiff peaks, and fold into batter. Pour over apples and bake 35 minutes or until cake tests done. Cool for 5 minutes. Loosen sides, if needed, and invert onto a serving plate. Let stand for 1 minute before removing pan. Serve warm.

Recipes by Dennis Vossel,
Glendale Heights, IL

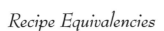

Recipe Equivalencies

3 Teaspoons = 1 Tablespoon
8 Tablespoons = ½ Cup
48 Teaspoons = 1 Cup

Stevia Powder (Green)
8–10 times sweeter than sugar
Replace 1 cup of sugar with 1½ to 2 tablespoons of Stevia.*

Stevia Extract Powder (White)
200–250 times sweeter than sugar
Replace one cup of sugar with approximately ¼ teaspoon of Stevia Extract.*

*Results may vary, depending on the brand and grade of the product used.

CHAPTER TEN

Questions and Answers

Q) What is Stevia?

A) Stevia Rebaudiana is an herb in the Chrysanthemum family which grows wild as a small shrub in parts of Paraguay and Brazil. The glycosides in its leaves, including up to 10% Stevioside, account for its incredible sweetness, making it unique among the nearly 300 species of Stevia plants.

There are indications that Stevia (or Ca-he-he) has been used to sweeten a native beverage called maté since Pre-Columbian times. However, a Natural Scientist names Antonio Bertoni first recorded its usage by native tribes in 1887.

Q) How much Stevia is used around the world?

A) Exact numbers are unavailable at this time. However, as an indication, Japanese consumers used the equivalent of 700 metric tonnes of Stevia leaves in 1987 alone. This number does not include other major consuming countries such as Brazil and the whole of South America; South Korea, China and the whole of the Pacific Rim; as well as Europe, Australia and North America. I would also assume that the Japanese figure has increased since 1987.

Q) What is the FDA's position on Stevia?

A) The FDA's position on Stevia is somewhat ambiguous. In 1991, citing a preliminary mutagenicity study, the FDA issued an import alert which effectively blocked the importation and sale of Stevia in this country. Ironically, this was the year that a follow-up study found flaws in the first study and seriously questioned its results.

In September of 1995, the FDA revised its import alert to allow Stevia and its extracts to be imported as a food supplement but not as a sweetener. Yet, it defines Stevia as an unapproved food additive, not affirmed as GRAS (Generally Recognized as Safe) in the United States. The following is a portion of this revised alert:

"If Stevia is to be used in a dietary supplement for a technical effect, such as use as a sweetener or flavoring agent, and is labeled as such, it is considered an unsafe food additive. However, in the absence of labeling specifying that stevia is being or will be used for technical effect, use of stevia as a dietary ingredient in a dietary supplement is not subject to the food additive provisions of FD & C ACT."

In my opinion, this revision represents a political compromise between the artificial sweetener and sugar lobbyists and the Natural Food Industry and its representatives, as mediated by the FDA.

Q) Where is Stevia cultivated?

A) Mainly in Paraguay, Brazil, Japan and China. There are other growers scattered across the Pacific Rim. Stevia is also being cultivated in Southern Ontario and Mexico. Surprisingly, it has been successfully grown in California and the South of England as well.

Q) How has Stevia been used in food applications?

A) First, as a prepackaged replacement for sugar and artificial sweeteners. Second, it has been used in various food products, including the Japanese sugar-free versions of Wrigley's gums, Beatrice Foods yogurts and even diet Coke. It has also been used in Japanese style pickles, dried seafoods, fish meat products, vegetables and seafoods boiled down with soy sauce, confectioneries and a host of other products. Whether it will reach into food applications such as these in the U.S. market will depend largely on the FDA's regulatory position and health industry efforts to re-classify Stevia as a GRAS (generally recognized as safe) substance.

Q) *Is Stevia safe?*

A) See chapter 6 for a detailed discussion. In general, Stevia is an all-natural herbal product with centuries of safe usage by native Indians in Paraguay. It has been thoroughly tested in dozens of tests around the world and found to be completely non-toxic. It has also been consumed safely in massive quantities (Thousands of tonnes annually) for the past twenty years. Although one group of studies, performed in 1985 through 1987, found one of the metabolites of steviosides, called Steviol, to be mutagenic towards a particular strain of Salmonella bacteria, there is serious doubt as to whether this study is applicable to human metabolism of Stevia. In fact, the methodology used to measure the mutagenicity in this test was flawed according to a follow-up piece of research which also seriously questioned the validity of the results. For myself, I intend to use the product with both confidence in nature and respect for the healthy moderation and balance which nature teaches us.

Q) *Can Stevia replace sugar in the diet?*

A) Yes. Refined sugar is virtually devoid of nutritional benefits and, at best, represents empty calories in the diet. At worst, it has been implicated in numerous degenerative diseases. Stevia is much sweeter than sugar and has none of sugar's unhealthy drawbacks.

Q) *How sweet is Stevia?*

A) The crude Stevia leaves and herbal powder (green) are reported to be 10–15 times sweeter than table sugar. The refined extracts of Stevia called steviosides (a white powder, 85-95% Steviosides) claim to be 200–300 times sweeter than table sugar. My experience is that the herbal powder is very sweet while the refined extract is *incredibly* sweet and needs to be diluted to be properly used. Both products have a slight bitter aftertaste, also characteristic of licorice.

Q) *Can Stevia replace artificial sweeteners in the diet?*

A) Yes! I do not believe that humans should consume anything artificial in their diets. Stevia offers a safe, all-natural, alternative to these "toxic time-bombs." And industrial usage in Japan proves that this substitution is both practical and economical.

Q) *How many calories are in Stevia?*

A) Virtually none. And the refined Stevia extracts are considered to be non-caloric.

Q) *Will Stevia raise my blood sugar levels?*

A) Not at all. In fact, according to some research, it may actually lower blood sugar levels. However, this research has yet to be confirmed and contradictory results make any conclusions premature.

Q) *Can I use Stevia if I am diabetic?*

A) Diabetes is a medical condition which should be monitored and treated by a qualified physician or health care practitioner. However, Stevia can be a part of a healthy diet for anyone with blood sugar problems since it does not raise blood sugar levels. If in doubt, ask your doctor. However, if they do say *no*, ask them *politely* for the current research to support their opinion.

Q) *Can I combine Stevia with other sweeteners?*

A) Most certainly. However, sweeteners in general should be used in moderation in a balanced healthy diet. And refined and artificial sweeteners should be avoided altogether.

Q) *Will Stevia harm my teeth?*

A) Apparently not. Two tests conducted by Purdue University's Dental Science Research Group have concluded that Stevioside is both fluoride compatible and "significantly" inhibits the development of plaque, thus Stevia may actually help to prevent cavities.

Q) Can Stevia be used in cooking and baking?

A) Absolutely! Industrial research in Japan has shown that Stevia and Stevioside extracts are extremely heat stable in a variety of everyday cooking and baking situations.

Q) Does Stevia contain vitamins and minerals?

A) Raw herbal Stevia contains nearly one hundred identified phytonutrients and volatile oils, including trace amounts of Rutin (from the Callus) and B-Sitosterol (from the leaves). However, in the quantities typically consumed, the nutritive benefits will be negligible. The extracts of Stevia, being more refined, will contain far fewer of these phytonutrients and volatile oils.

Q) How are Stevia extracts prepared?

A) Extracts of Stevia leaves can be prepared by a number of methods, some of which are patented. One researcher states: "Production of Stevioside involves water extraction from the dried leaves, followed by clarification and crystalization processes. Most commercial processes consist of water extraction, decoloration, and purification using ion-exchange resins, electrolytic techniques, or precipitating agents."

Q) Can I make my own Stevia Extract?

A) Yes. A liquid extract can be made from the whole Stevia leaves or from the green herbal Stevia powder. Simply combine a measured portion of Stevia leaves or herbal powder with pure USP grain alcohol (Brandy or Scotch will also do) and let the mixture sit for 24 hours. Filter the liquid from the leaves or powder residue and dilute to taste using pure water. Note that the alcohol content can be reduced by very slowly heating (not boiling) the extract and allowing the alcohol to evaporate off. A pure water extract can be similarly prepared, but will not extract quite as much of the sweet glycosides as will the alcohol. Either liquid extract can be cooked down and concentrated into a syrup.

Q) What is the replacement factor for Stevia herbal powder and extract in terms of common table sugar?

A) Since Stevia is 10 to 15 times sweeter than sugar, this is a fair, if approximate, replacement factor. Since the crude herb may vary in strength, some experimentation may be necessary. The high stevioside extracts are between 200–300 times sweeter than sugar and should be used sparingly. Unfortunately, FDA labelling guidelines may prevent manufacturers from providing a specific replacement factor.

Q) *What can't I do with Stevia?*

A) Stevia does not caramelize as sugar does. Meringues may also be difficult since Stevia does not brown or crystalize as sugar does.

Q) *Will Stevia change the color of my food?*

A) The green herbal powder may impart a slight amount of color to your food, depending on how much you use in your recipe. If you are concerned about color, I would suggest that you use the white powdered extract or a similar "clear" liquid extract of Stevia.

Q) *Where can I buy Stevia herbal powder and extract?*

A) At your local natural food store. As Stevia gains consumer acceptance, it may also begin to appear in supermarkets and grocery stores, but probably only in its refined form.

Q) *What is the future of Stevia?*

A) Very bright, as long as the gene stock of the Native Paraguay Stevia Rebaudiana species is preserved in the wild. Overharvesting and foreign transplantation has depleted this stock which contains the greatest possible gene diversity, essential to the strength and continuance of the species.

Q) *Can I grow my own stevia?*

A) Yes. Stevia grows as an annual in most parts of the United States and temperate regions of Canada. I suggest you buy stevia seedlings from one of the mail order sources listed in Appendix I or at a local greenhouse. Plant the seedlings after the first frost date in your area and 'harvest' the leaves before the first fall frost. Be sure to keep the plants moist but not inundated. See chapter 8 for detailed instruction.

CHAPTER ELEVEN

Stevia Products on the Market

1. **Stevia Leaves** • These are the whole leaves of the Stevia Rebaudiana plant, containing 8–12% sweet glycosides typically. These include Stevioside (5–8%) and Reboudioside A (1%) in addition to four other sweet constituents of Stevia.

2. **Stevia, Cut and Sifted** • The Stevia leaves are cut into smaller pieces and sifted for twigs and other extraneous matter.

3. **Stevia Powder** • The leaves are ground into a fine green powder, usually 80 to 100 mesh. This powder is typically 10–15 times sweeter than sugar.

4. **Stevia Extract 40–50% Sweet Glycosides** • The Stevia leaves are processed through one of several herbal extractive procedures, usually water or ethyl alcohol based. The resulting powder, usually off-white, contains 40-50% sweet glycosides and is more than one hundred times sweeter than sugar. The spectrum of glycosides results in a more "full" taste than pure Stevioside.

5. **Stevia Extract 85–95%** • The same as above, except of greater concentration. This pure white powder, more typically seen in the U.S. than the 40-50% extract, is between 200-300 times sweeter than sugar.

6. **Stevioside** • An isolated extract from the Stevia plant. This white powder typically contains over 90% Stevioside and is considered, scientifically, more pure than the "crude" extracts of 4 and 5. However, from a nutritional point of view, it is the most highly-processed and denatured of the above.

7. **Stevia Liquid Extracts** • Usually in a water and alcohol base, these extracts may be created from any of the previously mentioned forms of Stevia. As a result, color and strength may vary considerably.

8. **Other Stevia Glycoside Extracts** • Eight other sweet-tasting constituents of Stevia Rebaudiana have been identified in addition to Stevioside. These are Rebaudiosides A, B, C, D and E, Dulcosides A and B and Steviolbioside. While these have been isolated in the laboratory, only Rebaudiosides A has been widely extracted due to its relative abundance and its reported superior taste quality. However, this isolated extract is more expensive than extracts of Stevioside, and I have not yet seen it in the U.S. market.

9. **Stevia Seedlings.** Available from a limited number of herb growers and greenhouses. These 3-6" plants represent the easiest way to grow your own stevia. Note that stevia seeds are difficult to germinate.

Stevia Sources

Sources for Stevia powders and liquids

NOW Foods (wholesale)
395 S. Glen Ellyn Road
Bloomingdale, IL 60108
800-999-8069

Herbal Select
Unit 2, 355 Michener Road
Guelph, Ontario
Canada
888-313-3369

Sources for live Stevia rebaudiana plants

Canterbury Farms
16185 SW 108th Ave.
Tigard OR 97224
(503) 968-8269

Johnny's Selected Seeds (seeds)
Corn Shop Road
Unity, ME 04988
207-437-9294

Herbal Advantage, Inc.
Rt. 3, Box 93
Rogersville MO 65742
(800) 753-9199

Mountain Valley Growers
38325 Pepperweed Rd.
Squaw Valley CA 93675
(559) 338-2775

Mulberry Creek HerbFarm
3312 Bogart Rd.
Huron OH 44839
(419) 433-6126

One Green World
28696 South Cramer Rd.
Molalla OR 97038
(503) 651-3005

Pinetree Garden Seeds (seeds)
616A Lewiston Road
New Gloucester, ME 04260
207-926-4112

Richter's Herbs
Goodwood, ON L0C 1A0
Canada
(905) 640-6677

Sunnyboy Gardens
3314 Earlysville Rd.
Earlysville VA 22936
(804) 974-7350

Bibliography

Akashi, Haruo. "Safety of Dried Leaves Extracts of Stevia." *Abstract from Shokuhin Kogya.* Vol. 18, No. 20, October (1975).

Bakal, Abraham I. and Nabors, Lyn O'Brien. "Stevioside." *Alternative Sweeteners.* (1986), pp. 295-307.

Bracht, Ana Kelmer; Alvarez, Mauro, and Bracht, Adelar. "Effects of Stevia Rebaudiana Natural Products on Rat Liver Mitochondria." *Biochemical Pharmacology.* Vol. 34, No. 6, pp. 873-882, (1985).

Brandle, J.E. and Rosa, N. "Heritability for Yield, Leaf:Stem Ratio and Stevioside Content Estimated from a Landrace Cultivar of Stevia Rebaudiana." *Canadian Journal of Plant Science.* 72, pp. 1263-1266 (1992)

Brandle, J.E.; Starratt, A.N.; Gijzen, M. "Stevia rebaudiana: Its biological, chemical and agricultural properties." *Canadian Journal of Plant Science.* 78, pp 527-536 (1998).

Columbus, Mike. "The Cultivation of Stevia, 'Nature's Sweetener'." *Food and Rural Affairs Factsheet.* Ontario Ministry of Agriculture, May (1997).

Crammer, B. and Ikan, R. "Progress in the Chemistry and Properties of Rebaudiosides." *Developments in Sweeteners-3.* Elsevier Applied Science, London and New York, (1982). pp. 45-64.

Curi, R.; Alvarez, M.; Bazotte, R.B.; Botion, L.M.; Goday, J.L. and Bracht, A. "Effect of Stevia Rebaudiana on Glucose Tolerance in Normal Adult

Humans." *Brazilian Journal of Medical and Biological Research*. (1986), 19, pp. 771-774.

Darise, Muchsin; Kohda, Hiroshi; Mizutani, Kenji; Kasai, Ryoji and Tanaka, Osamu. "Chemical Constitutents of Flowers of Stevia Rebaudiana Bertoni." *Agricultural Biology and Chemistry*. 47 (1), pp. 133-135, (1983).

Ferreira, Claudio Martins and Handro, Walter. "Micro- propagation of Stevia Rebaudiana through Leaf Explants from Adult Plants." *Planta Medica*. (1988), pp. 157-160.

Fletcher, Hewitt G. Jr. "The Sweet Herb of Paraguay." *Plant Taxonomy*. July-August (1955), pp. 7, 18.

Fujita, Hideo and Edahiro, Tomoyoshi. "Safety and Utilization of Stevia Sweetener." *Shokumin Kogyo*, 22 (20), pp. 65-72. (1979).

Hoyle, Frances C. "Stevia Rebaudiana." *A Review of Four Potential New Crops for Australian Agriculture*. Division of Plant Industries. Technical Report No. 42, January (1992).

Ishidate, M. Jr.; Sofuni, T; Yashikawa, K.; Hayashi, M.;Nohmi, T.; Sawada, M. and Matsuoka, A. "Primary Mutagenicity Screening of Food Additives Currently Used in Japan." *Fd. Chem. Tox*. Vol. 22, No. 8, pp. 623-636.

Ishii, Emily L.; Schwab, Andreas and Bracht, Adelar. "Inhibition of Monosaccharide Transport in the Intact Rat Liver By Stevioside." Biochemical Pharmalocology. Vol. 36, No. 9, pp. 1417-1433, (1987).

Ishii, Emy L. and Bracht, Adelar. "Stevioside, the Sweet Glycoside of Stevia Rebaudiana, Inhibits the Action of Atractyloside in the Isolated Perfused Rat Liver." *Research Communications in Chemical Pathology and Pharmacology*. Vol, 53, No. 1, July (1986), pp 79-91.

Kazuyama, Seiichi. "Present Status of Natural Sweeteners from Stevia." *The Food and its Chemistry*. (1979), 21 (4), pp.90-94.

Kelmer-Bracht, Ana M.; Kemmelmeir, Fumie S.; Ishii, Emy L.; Alvarez, Mauro and Bracht, Adelar. "Effect of Stevia Rebaudiana Natural Products on Cellular and Sub-Cellular Metabolism." *Arg. Biol. Technology*. 28 (3) (1985), pp. 431-455.

Kinghorn, Douglas A. and Soejarto, Djaja D. "Current Status of Stevioside as a Sweetening Agent for Human Use." *Economic and Medicinal Plant Research*. Volume I. Academic Press Inc. (London) Ltd. (1985).

Kinghorn, Douglas A. and Soejarto, Doel D. "Stevioside." *Alternative Sweeteners.* 2nd Edition, (1991), pp. 157-170.

Kioniaki, Abe and Sonobe, Masaru. "Use of Stevioside in the Food Industry." *New Food Industry.* (1977), 19 (1), pp. 67-72.

Kohda Hiroshi; Kasai, Ryoh; Yamasaki, Kazuo; Murakami, Kuniko and Tanaka, Osamu. "New Sweet Diterpene Glucosides from Stevia Rebaudiana." *Phytochemistry.* (1976), Vol. 15, pp. 981-983.

Lee, Sang Jik; Lee, Rang Kap; Park Jyung Rewng; Kim, Kwang Soo and Tchai, Bum Suk. "A Study on the Safety of Stevioside as a New Sweetening Agent." Dept. of Food and Nutrition, Yeunguam University, Daegu Institute of Reproductive Medicine and Population, Seoul National University, (1979).

Lewis, Walter, L. "Notes on Economic Plants." *Economic Botany* 46 (3), pp. 336-340, (1992).

Melis, M.S. "Stevioside Effect on Renal Function of Normal and Hypertensive Rats," *Journal of Ethnopharmacology.* 36 (1992) pp. 213-217, Elsevier Scientific Publishers, Ireland Ltd.

Melis, M.S. and Sainati, A.R. "Effect of Calcium and Verpamil on Renal Function of Rats during Treatment with Stevioside." *Journal of Ethnopharmacology.* 33 (1991) pp. 257-261, Elsevier Scientific Publishers, Ireland Ltd.

Metivier, Jacques and Viana, Ana Maria. "The Effect of Long and Short Day Length upon the Growth of Whole Plants and Level of Soluble Proteins, Sugars and Stevioside in Leaves of Stevia Rebaudiana Bertoni." *Journal of Experimental Botany.* Vol 30, No. 119, pp. 1211-1222, December, (1979).

Murofushi, Noboru; Shigematsa, Yoshio; Nagura, Shigehiro and Takahashi, Nobutaka. "Metabolism of Steviol and its Derivatives by Gibberella Fujikovoi." *Agricultural Biology and Chemistry.* 46 (9), 2305-2311, (1982).

Nakayama, Kunio; Kasahara, Daigo and Yamamoto, Fumihiro. "Absorption, Distribution, Metabolism and Excretion of Stevioside in Rats." *Journal of the Food Hygenic Society of Japan.* Vol. 27, No. 1, pp. 1-8 (1986).

Oddone, Blas. *Technical Manual on 'How to Grow Stevia.'* Guarani Botanicals, Inc. Pawcatuck, Connecticut. (1997).

Peterson, Natasha. "Industry Unites to Solve FDA Riddles Over Stevia." *Natural Food Merchandiser.* April (1995), pp. 1, 22.

Pezzuto, John M.; Compadre, Cesar M; Swanson, Steven M.; Nanayakkara, N.P. Dhammika and Kinghorn, Douglas A. "Metabolic Activated Steviol, the Aglycone of Stevioside, is Mutagenic." *Proc. of the National Academy of Sciences.* Vol. 82, pp. 2478-2482, (April 1985).

Pezzuto, John M. "Chemistry, Metabolism and Biological Activity of Steviol..., the Aglycone of Stevioside." *New Trends in Natural Products Chemistry.* (1986), pp. 371-386.

Pezzuto, John M.; Nanayakkara, N.P. Dhammiki; Compadre, Cesar M.; Swanson, Steven M.; Kinghorn, Douglas A.; Guenther, Thomas M.; Sparnins, Vetta L. and Lam, Luke K.T. "Characterization of Bacterial Mutagenicity Mediated by 13-Hydroxy-ent-Kaurenoic Acid (Steviol) and Several Structurally Related Derivatives...." *Mutation Research.* 169, pp. 93-103, (1985).

Planas, Gladys Mezzei and Kuc, Joseph. "Contraceptive Properties of Stevia Rebaudiana." *Science,* Vol. 162, No. 3857, Nov.(1968), p. 1007.

Procinska, Emily; Bridges, Bryn A.; Hanson, James, R. "No Evidence for Direct-Acting Mutagenesis by 15-Oxosteviol a Possible Metabolite of Steviol." Short communication from the School of Molecular Sciences and MRC Cell Mutation Unit, University of Sussex, Palmer, Brighton, U.K., (1990).

Rajbhandari, Amriteswori and Roberts, Margaret F. "The Flavonoids of Stevia Rebaudiana." *Journal of Natural Products.* 46, pp. 194, 195, (1983).

Sadler, Lynda. "Stevia Allowable As A Dietary Supplement/Ingredient-Import Alert Revised." *Bulletin of the American Herbal Products Association.* Sept. 26, (1995).

Shigematsu, Yoshio; Murofushi, Noboru and Takahashi, Nobutaka. "Structures of the Metabolites from Steviol Methyl Ester by Gibberella Fujikuroi." *Agricultural Biological Chemistry.* 46 (9), 2313-2318, (1982).

Shock, Clinton L. "Experimental Cultivation of Rebaudi's Stevia in California." *Agronomy Progress Report.* University of California, Davis, April (1982).

Soejarto, D.D.; Compadre, C.M.; Medon, P.J.; Kamath, S.K. and Kinghorn, A.D. "Potential Sweetening Agents of Plant Origin II. Field Search for Sweet-Tasting Stevia Species." *Economic Botany.* 37 (1), (1983), pp. 71-79.

Sumida, Tetsuya. "Studies on Stevia rebaudiana Bertoni as a New Possible Crop for Sweetening Resource in Japan." *Journal of the Central Agricultural Station.* 31, 67-71 (1980).

Tanaka, Osuma, "Steviol-Glycosides: New Natural Sweeteners." *Alternative Sweeteners.* Marcel Dekker, Inc. (1986), New York, New York.

Tezuki, Shichigoro; Yamano, Toshiyuki; Shitou, Takeo and Tadouchi, Nobuo. "Determination of Sweetener in Sugarless Chewing Gum." (Central Research Laboratories Lotte Co., Ltd., Japan), Shokahin Kogyol, (1980).

Yamada, Akio; Sumiko, Ohgaki; Nada, Tsutomu and Shimizu, Mitsura. "Chronic Toxicity Study of Dietary Stevia Extracts in F344 Rats." *Journal of Food Hygiene Society of Japan.* Vol. 26, No. 2, pp. 169-183, (1984).

Zeaviu, Edna. "The Outlaw Herbal Sweetener." *East-West Journal.* February (1988), pp. 28-31.